CATECHISM

D1213233

CATECHISM

CHRISTIAN DOCTRINE
OF THE EVANGELICAL LUTHERAN
CHURCH OF FINLAND

Approved
in the General Synod
1999

EDITA, HELSINKI

The General Synod of the Evangelical Lutheran Church of Finland on 7 May 1993 requested that the Bishops' Conference take action on the drawing up of a new book on the basic truths of the Christian faith. In its spring session 1995, the Bishops' Conference called upon Bishop Eero Huovinen to write a proposal for this new book on Christian doctrine.

The drafting process lasted for three years. A fairly large group was assigned to read the drafts, give detailed written feedback, and meet regularly to comment on the text. From this group, a two-person team, consisting of a journalist, Mrs. Leena Huima, and a theologian, the Rev. Matti Poutiainen, assisted in the production of the text.

The draft was submitted to the Bishops' Conference, which forwarded its own proposal, based on Bishop Huovinen's draft, to the General Synod. After minor revision, the Finnish and Swedish versions of the new book on Christian doctrine were approved by the General Synod on 12 November 1999. The translation into English is by Riitta and Thomas Toepfer.

The Scripture portions quoted are from the New Revised Standard Version of the Bible. Attempt was made in the Ten Commandments, Creed, and Lord's Prayer to approach the language of the ICEL texts, with some changes called for due to the Finnish text of these. In particular, the Lord's Prayer uses "sins" rather than "debts" or "trespasses," and it follows the more traditional English form.

The Catechism is divided into numbered sections which follow the division of Martin Luther's Small Catechism. Each section of the catechism is divided into three parts: first, an explanatory text; secondly, Bible selections appropriate to that section; and, thirdly, the corresponding portion from Luther's Small Catechism (Tappert; some prayers: other sources).

EDITORIAL COMMITTEE

Graphic design and layout: Petteri Kivekäs
Photographs used in the illustrations: The Finnish Nature Photo Agency

ISBN 951-37-3330-0

Oy Edita Ab
Vilppula 2001, Finland

DEAR READER

The purpose of the Catechism is to state in a concise and clear format what the Christian faith is. Its deepest mission is to lead us to live our lives in faith to God and in love to one another.

The Ten Commandments, the Apostles' Creed and the Lord's Prayer are the inner core of the Catechism. We share them with Christians from a great many churches. In accordance with the *Small Catechism* of Martin Luther, this Catechism also presents the meaning of the sacraments of Baptism and Holy Communion, together with a few other essential issues.

The Ten Commandments express the fundamental law of life, that is what we are to do and what to leave undone. The Creed, further, tells us who God is, what he has done for us, and what he bestows upon us. The Lord's Prayer, moreover, directs us to prayer to God in order that we might cling to him in faith and live according to his will. The sacrament of Baptism is the bedrock of our spiritual lives. Finally, the Holy Communion strengthens us to live in faith and love. The word of God, Absolution pronounced after Confession, prayer and the Benediction will carry us through life.

The Catechism is the spiritual manual for every home, which conveys in a compact form the most essential message of the Bible. It speaks to us and sustains us in the midst of our daily lives. Time and again, we can meditate upon what it specifically wants to tell us.

TABLE OF CONTENTS

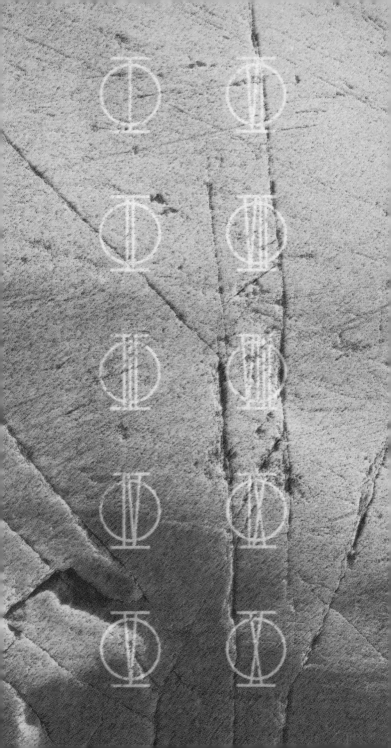

The Ten Commandments

1. I am the Lord your God.
You shall have no other gods.

2. You shall not take the name
of the Lord your God in vain.

3. Observe the sabbath day, to keep it holy.

4. Honor your father and your mother.

5. You shall not kill.

6. You shall not commit adultery.

7. You shall not steal.

8. You shall not bear false witness
against your neighbor.

9. You shall not covet
your neighbor's house.

10. You shall not covet your neighbor's wife,
or his workers, or his cattle,
or anything that is your neighbor's.

(Ex. 20:2-17; Deut. 5:6-21)

1

THE FIRST COMMANDMENT

I am the Lord your God. You shall have no other gods.

Knowing God is the most important and fundamental fact in our lives.

God approaches us in the midst of our lives, even though we do not always perceive it. Encountering God, we both fear and love him. The holiness of God arouses awe, whereas his love draws us towards him.

In his Commandments God shows us how we are to live our lives, while at the same time he reveals our selfishness and wickedness. The First Commandment inquires as to what we have built our lives on. Who or what is our god?

All people seek something to which they can attach their hope. We think that money, power and glory will protect us. We build our lives on a foundation of ourselves and our own deeds. Above all, we seek refuge in our own gods, who, however, are the reflections of our wishes and dreams. They cannot deliver what they promise.

The one refuge is God, who has created everything and who has stated that he is the God of all. His gifts are life and all the good that we have.

If we seek solace in our homespun idols, we turn away from God and his love. Since God is the giver of all good, our love belongs to him. He desires to be our one and only God.

■ Jesus said: "For where your treasure is, there will your heart be also." (Matt. 6:21)

■ You shall love the Lord your God with all your heart, and with all your soul, and with all your strength, and with all your mind; and your neighbor as yourself. (Luke 10:27)

I am the Lord your God. You shall have no other gods before me.

WHAT DOES THIS MEAN? ANSWER:

We should fear, love, and trust in God above all things.

(Martin Luther: Small Catechism)

2

THE SECOND COMMANDMENT

You shall not take the name of the Lord your God in vain.

God's name reminds us of who God is and what he desires, which arouses in us both unease and inexplicable longing. In all our adversities, we are to turn to him, awaiting his help. God has promised to hear us when in trust we call upon his name.

God's name is holy. We use his name correctly when we pray to him, when we give him honor and thanks. This is how we acknowledge him as our one and only God.

When we, in God's name or in reference to him, pursue our own selfish interests or subject other persons to us, we abuse his name. The mockery of God's name means despising God and a conscious turning away from him.

■ The Lord your God you shall fear; him you shall serve, and by his name alone you shall swear. (Deut. 6:13)

■ But God's firm foundation stands, bearing this inscription: "The Lord knows those who are his," and, "Let everyone who calls on the name of the Lord turn away from wickedness." (2 Tim. 2:19)

You shall not take the name of the Lord your God in vain.

WHAT DOES THIS MEAN? ANSWER:

We should fear and love God, and so we should not use his name to curse, swear, practise magic, lie, or deceive, but in every time of need to call upon him, pray to him, praise him, and give him thanks.

(Martin Luther: Small Catechism)

3

THE THIRD COMMANDMENT

Observe the sabbath day, to keep it holy.

God has given us both work and rest. Rest also includes things other than sleep and bodily rest. Pausing before God is the deepest meaning of the day of rest.

In quietude we sense the presence of the Holy, even though we might be able to give it neither name nor shape. Our own brokenness and the conflicts of life awaken in us questions, forcing us to seek answers to them.

The Holy God wishes to answer us. In his word he enters into our world and speaks our language. If we do not want to listen to him, we shut him out of our lives.

The divine service on the Lord's day is a meeting place where he talks to us and we talk to him. From God's Holy Word we learn to understand what he says to us and how he answers our prayers.

The setting aside of Sunday from the rest of the week also reminds us that we need a common day of rest. It is God's good will that each of us has the possibility to have a day of rest.

■ For in six days the Lord made heaven and earth, the sea, and all that is in them, but rested the seventh day; therefore the Lord blessed the sabbath day and consecrated it. (Ex. 20:11)

■ If you refrain from trampling the sabbath, from pursuing your own interests on my holy day; if you call the sabbath a delight and the holy day of the Lord honorable; if you honor it, not going your own ways, serving your own interests, or pursuing your own affairs; then you shall take delight in the Lord. (Is. 58:13–14)

■ Jesus said: "The sabbath was made for humankind, and not humankind for the sabbath; so the Son of Man is lord even of the sabbath." (Mark 2:27–28)

■ When he came to Nazareth, where he had been brought up, he went to the synagogue on the sabbath day, as was his custom. (Luke 4:16)

Remember the Sabbath day, to keep it holy.

WHAT DOES THIS MEAN? ANSWER:

We should fear and love God, and so we should not despise his Word and the preaching of the same, but deem it holy and gladly hear and learn it.

(Martin Luther: Small Catechism)

4

THE FOURTH COMMANDMENT

Honor your father and your mother.

It is God's will that every child have a father and a mother. They are entitled to special respect and honor because they are our parents.

It is the task of the parents to protect the child by tending to her wellbeing and rearing. Further, the parents are to guide the child in the knowledge of God and in love towards the neighbor. The child has both a need and the right to be granted the possibility of honoring the parents.

Although the parents wish the best for their children, their words and deeds may still be loveless and wrong. Even in a situation when we children decide to act contrary to our parents' will, we are to listen to them and honor them. This Commandment also urges adults to honor their aging parents and take care of them.

In society, public authority is entrusted to authorities whose responsibility it is to protect all citizens and see that justice is carried out. A good government is among God's best gifts. Being faithful to God is, however, more important than obeying people.

When we respect those who are entrusted with the responsibility of governing, we show confidence in God's care. God promises that this will also benefit us.

■ Listen to your father who begot you, and do not despise your mother when she is old. (Prov. 23:22)

■ Children, obey your parents in the Lord, for this is right. "Honor your father and mother"— this is the first commandment with a promise:"so that it may be well with you and you may live long on the earth." And, fathers, do not provoke your children to anger, but bring them up in the discipline and instruction of the Lord. (Eph. 6:1–4)

Honor your father and your mother.

WHAT DOES THIS MEAN? ANSWER:

We should fear and love God, and so we should not despise our parents and superiors, nor provoke them to anger, but honor, serve, obey, love, and esteem them.

(Martin Luther: Small Catechism)

5

THE FIFTH COMMANDMENT

You shall not kill.

Since God is love, he wants us to love our neighbors as ourselves.

Each person's life is a gift of God, and as such valuable. We must not cause our fellow human beings any harm or pain. On the contrary, we are to protect them in all circumstances. The very weakest in society are to be given special nurture.

The Commandment to love our fellow human concerns both individuals and society. When the government defends those whose lives or welfare are being threatened, it thereby promotes the fulfillment of love in society. For the common good, the government may have to use force to prevent the spreading of violence.

As individuals, we must not take justice in our own hands, but rather we are to forgive and to give up our desire for revenge. If we harm human life or other life around us, we set ourselves against God and his creative work.

■ Jesus said: "You have heard that it was said to those of ancient times, 'You shall not murder'; and 'whoever murders shall be liable to judgment.' But I say to you that if you are angry with a brother or sister, you will be liable to judgment; and if you insult a brother or sister, you will be liable to the council." (Matt. 5:21–22)

■ Beloved, never avenge yourselves, but leave room for the wrath of God; for it is written, "Vengeance is mine, I will repay, says the Lord." (Rom. 12:19)

■ Love does no wrong to a neighbor. (Rom. 13:10)

You shall not kill.

WHAT DOES THIS MEAN? ANSWER:

We should fear and love God, and so we should not endanger our neighbor's life, nor cause him any harm, but help and befriend him in every necessity of life.

(Martin Luther: Small Catechism)

6

THE SIXTH COMMANDMENT

You shall not commit adultery.

God has created us men and women. Sexuality is a part of God's creative work. Its purpose is to serve the initiation and preservation of the relationship between man and woman. In a marital relationship, we can bring joy to the spouse, learning to love in a serving manner and to rear a new generation.

Marriage is the foundation of the family. The family is protected by public commitment and societal endorsement. It is in lifelong marriage where the relationship between a woman and a man can be best fulfilled in the way God has intended.

The requirement of protecting marriage concerns both our own marriage and that of others. This demand covers the entire life span. Sexuality disconnected from love and from responsibility enslaves people, bringing harm to themselves and others.

The breach of the marriage brings wounds to our deepest human relationships, shattering the very foundation of life. The spouses' mutual forgiveness and willingness to commit themselves to one another may, however, help them out of this dead end situation. The final breakup of marriage may lead to divorce.

The decision to remarry is a responsible and serious one. To bring the new marriage before God

and people not only requires the will to recommit oneself but also involves mercy and forgiveness.

■ Did not one God make her? Both flesh and spirit are his. And what does the one God desire? Godly offspring. So look to yourselves, and do not let anyone be faithless to the wife of his youth. (Mal. 2:15)

■ Jesus said: "But from the beginning of creation, God made them male and female. For this reason a man shall leave his father and mother and be joined to his wife, and the two shall become one flesh. So they are no longer two, but one flesh. Therefore what God has joined together, let no one separate." (Mark 10:6–9)

You shall not commit adultery.

WHAT DOES THIS MEAN? ANSWER:

We should fear and love God, and so we should lead a chaste and pure life in word and deed, each one loving and honoring his wife or her husband.

(Martin Luther: Small Catechism)

7

THE SEVENTH COMMANDMENT

You shall not steal.

Money and possessions are God's good and necessary gifts, and yet they are the most common idols of humankind.

All things good created by God are meant for everyone. Love constrains us to look after the well-being of all humans. Our shared responsibility extends to all human beings. If we selfishly seek our own interest at the expense of the poor, we steal from those whose living conditions are the weakest. We are to be prepared to cut back on our personal as well as our national welfare and prosperity.

We are not to steal money or property or obtain it for ourselves deceitfully. The appropriation or destruction of common property is also theft. The exploitation of others, the failure to take responsibility for one's work, and also profiteering are all the acquisition of benefits at the expense of others. The destruction of the environment and the disruption of the balance of nature are stealing from future generations.

■ Swearing, lying, and murder, and stealing and adultery break out; bloodshed follows bloodshed. Therefore the land mourns, and all who live in it languish; together with the wild animals and the birds of the air, even the fish of the sea are perishing. (Hos. 4:2–3)

■ Thieves must give up stealing; rather let them labor and work honestly with their own hands, so as to have something to share with the needy. (Eph. 4:28)

You shall not steal.

WHAT DOES THIS MEAN? ANSWER:

We should fear and love God, and so we should not rob our neighbor of his money or property, nor bring them into our possession by dishonest trade or by dealing in shoddy wares, but help him to improve and protect his income and property.

(Martin Luther: Small Catechism)

8

THE EIGHTH COMMANDMENT

You shall not bear false witness against your neighbor.

It is God's will that we respect each other. Loving our neighbor also involves the protection of their reputation and honor, the loss of which is a hard blow whose impact may be felt throughout life.

We ourselves wish that only good things would be said about us. We are to speak of our neighbors in the way we want them to speak of us. If others spread negative messages about our neighbor, love calls upon us to support and help this neighbor.

The reputation of others is to be guarded both privately and publicly. Before matters can be made public, the requirements of justice and truth, together with openness, must be met. We are not, however, to reveal our neighbor's offenses without definite knowledge and adequate cause.

The assessment of offenses has been entrusted to the judicial system, which makes decisions as to the guilty parties and places them at responsibility for their deeds. In private life we are not to blame others or reveal their weaknesses. It is our task to encourage them to free themselves from their past and to seek new direction in their lives.

■ *You shall not spread a false report. You shall not join hands with the wicked to act as a malicious witness. You shall not follow a majority in wrongdoing; when you bear witness in a lawsuit, you shall not side with the majority so as to pervert justice. (Ex. 23:1–2)*

■ *Do not lie to one another, seeing that you have stripped off the old self with its practices and have clothed yourselves with the new self, which is being renewed in knowledge according to the image of its creator. (Col. 3:9–10)*

You shall not bear false witness against your neighbor.

WHAT DOES THIS MEAN? ANSWER:

We should fear and love God, and so we should not tell lies about our neighbor, nor betray, slander, or defame him, but should apologize for him, speak well of him, and interpret charitably all that he does.

(Martin Luther: Small Catechism)

9

THE NINTH COMMANDMENT

You shall not covet your neighbor's house.

The ninth and tenth Commandments are examples of how far both the demand of love and the dominion of selfishness extend. In them, everything stated in the previous commandments is expanded upon and deepened. God sees even our secret thoughts and extends his commandments to cover coveting as well.

We are to protect and defend our neighbors even if it means giving up our own rights. God forbids us to seek our own good at the expense of others, even if the means are legitimate.

The Commandments demand that we do right even when no law of society forces us to do so. The Commandments turn our eyes towards our own innermost beings and the ultimate reasons for our behavior.

The envying and coveting of other people's possessions, both visibly and in our secret thoughts, is always a sign of distrust of God. He wants us to put our trust in him only and to expect good things in life from him.

■ Alas for those who devise wickedness and evil deeds on their beds! When the morning dawns, they perform it, because it is in their power. They covet fields, and seize them; houses, and take them away; they oppress householder and house, people and their inheritance. (Mic. 2:1–2)

■ What then should we say? That the law is sin? By no means! Yet, if it had not been for the law, I would not have known sin. I would not have known what it is to covet if the law had not said, "You shall not covet." (Rom. 7:7)

You shall not covet your neighbor's house.

WHAT DOES THIS MEAN? ANSWER:

We should fear and love God, and so we should not seek by craftiness to gain possession of our neighbor's inheritance or home, nor to obtain them under pretext of legal right, but be of service and help to him so that he may keep what is his.

(Martin Luther: Small Catechism)

10

THE TENTH COMMANDMENT

**You shall not covet
your neighbor's wife, or his
workers, or his cattle, or anything
that is your neighbor's.**

The world created by God includes other things besides just earthly possessions. The people we live with and work with are important parts of our lives.

Each person's life has a meaning and a mission which is realized wherever we live and however we live, at any particular phase of our lives. We are to protect and give support to everything belonging to our neighbor's life. By following God's will, by using our own good judgment, and by placing ourselves in our neighbor's shoes, we continue to find new opportunities to do good. Innovative love seeks ways to serve in all situations.

The contents of the Commandments can be expressed by saying that we are to love God above everything and our neighbor as ourselves. We are to treat others as we wish to be treated ourselves.

■ Jesus said: "In everything do to others as you would have them do to you; for this is the law and the prophets." (Matt. 7:12)

■ The commandments, "You shall not commit adultery; You shall not murder; You shall not steal; You shall not covet"; and any other commandment, are summed up in this word, "Love your neighbor as yourself." (Rom. 13:9)

You shall not covet your neighbor's wife, or his manservant, or his maidservant, or his ox, or his cattle, or anything that is your neighbor's.

WHAT DOES THIS MEAN? ANSWER:

We should fear and love God, and so we should not abduct, estrange, or entice away our neighbor's wife, servants, or cattle, but encourage them to remain and discharge their duty to him.

(Martin Luther: Small Catechism)

11

THE COMMANDMENTS –
THE LAW OF LOVE

The Commandments express the conditions of a good life for everyone. The demand of love included in them is known to all religions and cultures. People understand that the Commandments express the law of life itself. The consequences of both breaking and obeying the Commandments reach far beyond the individual human being. Its effects are also reflected in families and societies from generation to generation.

Since God wills good to people, he expects unconditional love. The Commandments are not simply life principles, but they indicate that none of us are able to fulfill God's demands, even though our hearts do acknowledge them to be just. Something in us fights against God's loving will. Even in doing good we still seek our own interest. Except we have trust in God, the source of all goodness, we put our own well-being above all else. It is then that relations with other people are invalidated.

The Commandments show us that the most important and fundamental matter in our lives is faith in God.

■ He has told you, O mortal, what is good; and what does the Lord require of you but to do justice, and to love kindness, and to walk humbly with your God? (Mic. 6:8)

■ By this we know that we love the children of God, when we love God and obey his commandments. For the love of God is this, that we obey his commandments. And his commandments are not burdensome. (1 John 5:2–3)

WHAT DOES GOD DECLARE CONCERNING ALL THESE COMMANDMENTS? ANSWER:

He says, "I the Lord your God am a jealous God, visiting the iniquity of the fathers upon the children to the third and the fourth generation of those who hate me, but showing steadfast love to thousands of those who love me and keep my commandments."

WHAT DOES THIS MEAN? ANSWER:

God threatens to punish all who transgress these commandments. We should therefore fear his wrath and not disobey these commandments. On the other hand, he promises grace and every blessing to all who keep them. We should therefore love him, trust in him, and cheerfully do what he has commanded.

(Martin Luther: Small Catechism)

The Creed

I believe in God,
the Father, Almighty,
Creator of heaven and earth.

I believe in Jesus Christ, his only Son,
our Lord.
He was conceived by the power
of the Holy Spirit
and born of the virgin Mary.
He suffered under Pontius Pilate,
was crucified, died, and was buried.
He descended into hell.
On the third day he rose again.
He ascended into heaven,
and is seated at the right hand
of the Father.
He will come again to judge
the living and the dead.

I believe in the Holy Spirit,
the holy catholic Church,
the communion of saints,
the forgiveness of sins,
the resurrection of the body,
and the life everlasting.

12

I believe in God,

The creed briefly states what God gives us and what he does for us. We are incapable of fulfilling the demand of faith and of unconditional love contained in the commandments. Yet God gives us faith and opens our hearts to love.

Our reason cannot understand God. The depths of his being remain a secret even to Christian believers. God has, however, revealed to us all that is necessary for us to live in faith to him.

God approaches us as Creator, Redeemer, and Sanctifier. He is the Triune God: the Father, the Son, and the Holy Spirit. God has created everything. He has become as one of us in the Son, and he is present in the Holy Spirit. God is not merely some remote initial cause or nonpersonal force, but he works in creation and history, encountering us personally.

The Creed is the praise of God's good deeds. While we ask for faith for ourselves, we thank God for his infinite love. In faith we accept God's gifts and put our trust in him, holding on to his promises as true, daring to launch out on these promises. The communal faith of the Church supports us even then when our own faith wavers.

■ *Know that the Lord is God. It is he that made us, and we are his; we are his people, and the sheep of his pasture.* (Ps. 100:3)

■ *Jesus said: "Everyone therefore who acknowledges me before others, I also will acknowledge before my Father in heaven."* (Matt. 10:32)

13

the Father, Almighty,
Creator of heaven and earth.

God is the Creator of all. With his word he created the entire universe. Science studies the mystery of the genesis of the world as well as the evolution of nature and people. Faith trusts that underlying all is God's creative will and love for the creation.

God's good creative work is not confined to the genesis of the world and life. The creation is not in the hands of blind fate, for God himself continues to look out for it. The preservation of life, the realization of justice, and friendship between people are examples of the fact that God works in his creation and loves the created. Everything right, pure, and beautiful comes from him. Home and family, food and drink, health and rest are God's gifts.

As Creator, God is everyone's heavenly father. We are his children and live under his care. It is our duty to protect and look after God's world. We are held responsible to our Creator for carrying out this task.

The created world includes God's heaven. It is not within the reach of our senses in this life, but by faith we understand its existence. Angels were created by God to be the messengers of his will and love.

God's power is infinite and eternal. In the difficult times in history and in the problematic destinies of human lives, too, everything takes place because he wills it or allows it. Even when we do not understand or accept suffering, we can place our trust in our all-powerful Father.

■ In the beginning when God created the heavens and the earth.... (Gen. 1:1)

■ In the beginning was the Word, and the Word was with God, and the Word was God. He was in the beginning with God. All things came into being through him, and without him not one thing came into being. (John 1:1–3)

I believe in God, the father almighty, maker of heaven and earth.

WHAT DOES THIS MEAN? ANSWER:

I believe that God has created me and all that exists; that he has given me and still sustains my body and soul, all my limbs and senses, my reason and all the faculties of my mind, together with food and clothing, house and home, family and property; that he provides me daily and abundantly with all the necessities of life, protects me from all danger, and preserves me from all evil. All this he does out of his pure, fatherly, and divine goodness and mercy, without any merit or worthiness on my part. For all of this I am bound to thank, praise, serve, and obey him. This is most certainly true.

(Martin Luther: Small Catechism)

14

I believe in Jesus Christ, his only Son,

In Jesus, God's love became visible within this world. God took part in the human by sending his only Son to us.

Jesus was a historic figure, from the town of Nazareth. He was born, and he died. He rejoiced and grieved just as any of us. Jesus was a friend especially to those who were belittled and despised by others. This is how he gave witness to God's love toward all people. By his life Jesus showed what obedience to the Father's will meant.

God's Son was born in our likeness, to free us and to bear the judgment we deserved. He subjected himself to be one of us and shared the destiny of humankind enslaved to sin. Jesus is the suffering Messiah, that is, the Christ, awaited in the Old Testament.

Jesus Christ is true God and true man. As the only Son of God, he was different from other religious teachers. Even though he possesses all of God's power and strength, he does not remain distant in his glory but lives and reigns among us. In a world of despair, where the power of evil appears to be overwhelming, Christ is our only hope.

■ Jesus said: "For God so loved the world that he gave his only Son, so that everyone who believes in him may not perish but may have eternal life." (John 3:16)

■ If God is for us, who is against us? He who did not withhold his own Son, but gave him up for all of us, will he not with him also give us everything else? (Rom. 8:31–32)

15

our Lord.

Christ came into the world because of us and for our sakes. He is our Lord and Savior.

Sin separates us from God, the fountain of life. Each and every one of us is subjected to sin at birth, and none of us can free ourselves from it by our own power. We are incapable of loving God above everything and of loving our neighbors as ourselves.

Through his life, death, and resurrection, Jesus Christ has destroyed the power of sin, death, and Satan. They can no longer hold us as their own. Faith in Christ removes us from the bondage of Satan to the freedom of God's kingdom. Christ becomes our Lord. He gives himself to us, and we become partakers of his innocence, holiness, and love.

Christ rules as God, who consented to suffering. His kingship has no outward signs of power, but in his kingdom we are given freedom, peace, and joy.

■ If you confess with your lips that Jesus is Lord and believe in your heart that God raised him from the dead, you will be saved. (Rom. 10:9)

■ It is no longer I who live, but it is Christ who lives in me. (Gal. 2:20)

■ At the name of Jesus every knee should bend, in heaven and on earth and under the earth, and every tongue should confess that Jesus Christ is Lord, to the glory of God the Father. (Phil. 2:10–11)

16

He was conceived by the power of the Holy Spirit and born of the virgin Mary.

It is impossible to understand in a reasonable way how God became human. God hiding in the lowly and the mundane is an unfathomable miracle, visible and understandable only to faith.

The historicity of Jesus' birth and death is revealed through two names in the Creed, that is, Jesus was born of the virgin Mary and he died at the time of Pontius Pilate. Christianity is more than just a timeless ideology. It is a faith in God who manifested himself in the midst of human history.

Mary of Nazareth was obedient in that she consented to God's miracle, and so gave birth to Jesus. This is how she became the Mother of God. Mary's faith is a model for us. She trusted God even though she could not comprehend his plans and manner of working.

■ Mary said to the angel, "How can this be, since I am a virgin?" The angel said to her, "The Holy Spirit will come upon you, and the power of the Most High will overshadow you; therefore the child to be born will be holy; he will be called Son of God." (Luke 1:34–35)

■ Mary said, "My soul magnifies the Lord, and my spirit rejoices in God my Savior, for he has looked with favor on the lowliness of his servant. Surely, from now on all generations will call me blessed; for the Mighty One has done great things for me, and holy is his name. His mercy is for those who fear him from generation to generation." (Luke 1:46–50)

17

He suffered under Pontius Pilate, was crucified, died and was buried. He descended into hell.

Jesus suffered and died for us. He knew God's will and was subject to it even though it meant being imprisoned, ridiculed, and crucified. God's Son concealed his omnipotence and allowed himself to be sentenced to death with criminals.

On Calvary's cross Jesus cried out publicly his despair over the fact that God had forsaken him. He died alone and disgraced. His friends and family laid him to rest. Death seemed to have gained its final victory.

Jesus consented to be subjected to God's wrath on our behalf, taking upon himself, innocent, the punishment which we had earned for our sins. Thus Christ atoned for the sins of all humankind. He shed his blood as a sacrifice for each of us and redeemed us.

Jesus' death starts a new life. When he stepped into the kingdom of the dead, he demonstrated his power in the midst of all evil. Hidden within death on the cross, defeat, was victory over sin, death, and Satan.

■ [Christ,] though he was in the form of God, did not regard equality with God as something to be exploited, but emptied himself, taking the form of a slave, being born in human likeness. And being found in human form, he humbled himself and became obedient to the point of death—even death on a cross. (Phil. 2:6–8)

■ Christ said: "Do not be afraid; I am the first and the last, and the living one. I was dead, and see, I am alive forever and ever; and I have the keys of Death and of Hades." (Rev. 1:17–18)

18

On the third day he rose again.
He ascended into heaven,
and is seated at the right hand
of the Father. He will come again
to judge the living and the dead.

Death could not hold dominion over Christ. In accord with the prophecies of Scripture, he rose from the dead. On the first day of the week, the disciples saw an empty tomb and were confused. When they met their risen Lord, they began to understand what had taken place.

Christ's resurrection is a victory over death. Satan's power has been broken, so death does not have the last say. The overcomer of death also frees us from the other destructive forces of evil. Resurrection and eternal life await us.

Christ, who ascended into heaven, rules at the right hand of the Father almighty. We can no longer see Jesus the way his contemporaries did, but according to his promise he will always be among us. Christ prays for us. He knows our pain and our anxiety, having lived a human life.

At the end of time Christ will return. All will then have to bow to his power and righteous judgment. We are saved from everlasting perdition only by Christ's mercy. With confidence the Christian awaits the future and the day when Christ's kingdom becomes visible.

■ *Who is to condemn? It is Christ Jesus, who died, yes, who was raised, who is at the right hand of God, who indeed intercedes for us. (Rom. 8:34)*

■ *Now if Christ is proclaimed as raised from the dead, how can some of you say there is no resurrection of the dead? If there is no resurrection of the dead, then Christ has not been raised; and if Christ has not been raised, then our proclamation has been in vain and your faith has been in vain. (1 Cor. 15:12–14)*

And in Jesus Christ, his only son, our Lord: who was conceived by the Holy Spirit, born of the virgin Mary, suffered under Pontius Pilate, was crucified, dead, and buried: he descended into hell, the third day he rose again from the dead, he ascended into heaven, and is seated on the right hand of God, the Father almighty, whence he shall come to judge the living and the dead.

WHAT DOES THIS MEAN? ANSWER:

I believe that Jesus Christ, true God, begotten of the Father from eternity, and also true man, born of the virgin Mary, is my Lord, who has redeemed me, a lost and condemned creature, delivered me and freed me from all sins, from death, and from the power of the devil, not with silver and gold but with his holy and precious blood and with his innocent sufferings and death, in order that I may be his, live under him in his kingdom, and serve him in everlasting righteousness, innocence, and blessedness, even as he is risen from the dead and lives and reigns to all eternity. This is most certainly true.

(Martin Luther: Small Catechism)

19

I believe in the Holy Spirit,

Before his death, Jesus promised to send the Holy Spirit to defend and to guide his own. After the resurrection, at Pentecost, God poured out his Spirit upon the disciples and filled them with his grace and gifts.

The Holy Spirit brings God's goodness and Christ's love in our midst. Without the life-giving Spirit, we cannot believe in or approach Christ. We run away from God and turn our backs on him. The Holy Spirit calls us, creating faith and new life in us. He gives us Christ with all his gifts and protects us in the right faith.

According to his name, the Holy Spirit is the Sanctifier, who makes sinful people holy. He opens our hearts to hear God's word, to know Christ, and to trust in God's promises. Through the influence of the Holy Spirit, we become partakers of God's gifts of grace, and begin to love God and our neighbors.

■ Jesus said: "But the Advocate, the Holy Spirit, whom the Father will send in my name, will teach you everything, and remind you of all that I have said to you." (John 14:26)

■ The fruit of the Spirit is love, joy, peace, patience, kindness, generosity, faithfulness, gentleness, and self-control. (Gal. 5:22–23)

20

the holy catholic Church,

The Holy Spirit gathers the Christian Church and sanctifies it. The Church, the Christian congregation, is a community of pardoned sinners who trust in God and in whom the Holy Spirit awakens faith and love.

Since its inception, the Church has been called the Body of Christ. It is a living entity, whose head is Christ, and into which we enter through baptism. Although people are different, we do share a common faith that ties us to Christ and to one another. Further, the Church is depicted as a mother who carries us in her arms and nurtures us.

God's word, Baptism, and the Holy Communion are the visible signs of the church. These are called the means of grace since the Holy Spirit uses them as he communicates God's grace to us. In accordance with Christ's will, the Church calls and ordains servants of the word to administer the means of grace. With his word, God both examines us and pardons us. The task entrusted to all Christians is to proclaim the Gospel of Christ to the entire world.

■ *Now you are the body of Christ and individually members of it.* (1 Cor. 12:27)

■ *And he has put all things under his feet and has made him the head over all things for the church, which is his body, the fullness of him who fills all in all.* (Eph. 1:22–23)

21

the communion of saints,

The Christian Church is one, holy, catholic, and apostolic. The Church is one since it has one Lord and common faith. Secondly, the Church is holy because the Holy Spirit works in its midst. Thirdly, the Church is catholic, i.e. universal, since it has been sent to serve all nations with God's word. Finally, the Church is apostolic as it lives by the Gospel handed down by Jesus' first disciples.

The unity of Christians is not a uniformity of customs and human traditions. Neither is it created by a shared sentiment. The basis of our unity is the common faith in which we are joined by the Holy Spirit through the word and the sacraments. Throughout its history, the Christian Church has divided into diverse denominations and communities. Jesus' prayer that his followers might be one obliges us to seek unity in faith and love.

The Christian Church carries out its mission in the midst of human life. Each and every one of us is invited to the fellowship of our respective parishes. The faith we share joins us to the Church universal of Christ, gathered by the Holy Spirit from all nations.

■ Jesus said: "I ask not only on behalf of these, but also on behalf of those who will believe in me through their word, that they may all be one. As you, Father, are in me and I am in you, may they also be in us, so that the world may believe that you have sent me." (John 17:20–21)

■ There is no longer Jew or Greek, there is no longer slave or free, there is no longer male and female; for all of you are one in Christ Jesus. (Gal. 3:28)

■ … making every effort to maintain the unity of the Spirit in the bond of peace. There is one body and one Spirit, just as you were called to the one hope of your calling, one Lord, one faith, one baptism, one God and Father of all, who is above all and through all and in all. (Eph. 4:3–6)

22

the forgiveness of sins,

Because of Christ's redeeming work, God forgives all repentant sinners. He will no longer remember our evil but loves us as his children.

The Christian, however, remains a sinner to the end of life, so we all have to put our trust in God's mercy daily, as none can rid ourselves of the evil that rules in our lives. At one and the same time, we are altogether sinners, and yet on account of Christ, altogether righteous, meaning acceptable to God.

As God forgives us our sins, he awakens in us new life. He strengthens our faith and increases our love to our neighbors. We need not be hopeless even though we discover in ourselves unbelief and evil. God promises that he will continue the work that he started in us.

■ Bless the Lord, O my soul, and do not forget all his benefits—who forgives all your iniquity, who heals all your diseases, who redeems your life from the Pit, who crowns you with steadfast love and mercy. (Ps. 103:2–4)

■ When Jesus saw their faith, he said, "Friend, your sins are forgiven you." (Luke 5:20)

■ Jesus said: "... they may receive forgiveness of sins and a place among those who are sanctified by faith in me." (Acts 26:18)

■ If we confess our sins, he who is faithful and just will forgive us our sins and cleanse us from all unrighteousness. (1 John 1:9)

23

the resurrection of the body,

In the hour of death, we will have to give up the temporal life God has given us. The destructive forces of evil will seem to overcome us. Our bodies will decay, but our souls will await the day of resurrection when both the living and the dead are gathered before God for judgment.

For a Christian believer, death is the gateway to the life to come. With confidence, we can rest in our Heavenly Father's arms, since Christ has already conquered death. The Son of God has risen from the dead before us. We, too, will have new immortal bodies fashioned after Christ's resurrection body. In this way God's original creative work will be carried out in us.

■ Jesus said: "Do not be astonished at this; for the hour is coming when all who are in their graves will hear his voice and will come out—those who have done good, to the resurrection of life, and those who have done evil, to the resurrection of condemnation." (John 5:28–29)

■ And as for what you sow, you do not sow the body that is to be, but a bare seed, perhaps of wheat or of some other grain. But God gives it a body as he has chosen, and to each kind of seed its own body. So it is with the resurrection of the dead. What is sown is perishable, what is raised is imperishable. It is sown in dishonor, it is raised in glory. It is sown in weakness, it is raised in power. It is sown a physical body, it is raised a spiritual body. If there is a physical body, there is also a spiritual body. (1 Cor. 15:37–38, 42–44)

■ But we do not want you to be uninformed, brothers and sisters, about those who have died, so that you may not grieve as others do who have no hope. For since we believe that Jesus died and rose again, even so, through Jesus, God will bring with him those who have died. (1 Thess. 4:13–14)

24

and the life everlasting.

Jesus has promised that no one who believes in him will ever die. Those trusting God already live out eternal life in this time. Yet, we only comprehend eternity inadequately during our lives on this earth.

One day we will see God face to face. With him we will have a life without suffering and pain. God will create the new heavens and the new earth where there is no evil. Together with all the saints we will serve God and rejoice in his eternal love.

■ *Jesus said: "Very truly, I tell you, anyone who hears my word and believes him who sent me has eternal life, and does not come under judgment, but has passed from death to life." (John 5:24)*

■ *Jesus said: "I am the resurrection and the life. Those who believe in me, even though they die, will live, and everyone who lives and believes in me will never die." (John 11:25–26)*

■ *For the wages of sin is death, but the free gift of God is eternal life in Christ Jesus our Lord. (Rom. 6:23)*

■ *See, the home of God is among mortals. He will dwell with them; they will be his peoples, and God himself will be with them; he will wipe every tear from their eyes. Death will be no more; mourning and crying and pain will be no more, for the first things have passed away. (Rev. 21:3–4)*

I believe in the Holy Spirit, the holy Christian church, the communion of saints, the forgiveness of sins, the resurrection of the body, and the life everlasting. Amen.

WHAT DOES THIS MEAN? ANSWER:

I believe that by my own reason or strength I cannot believe in Jesus Christ, my Lord, or come to him. But the Holy Spirit has called me through the Gospel, enlightened me with his gifts, and sanctified and preserved me in true faith, just as he calls, gathers, enlightens, and sanctifies the whole Christian church on earth and preserves it in union with Jesus Christ in the one true faith. In this Christian church he daily and abundantly forgives all my sins, and the sins of all believers, and on the last day he will raise me and all the dead and will grant eternal life to me and to all who believe in Christ. This is most certainly true.

(Martin Luther: Small Catechism)

The Lord's Prayer

Our Father, who art in heaven.
Hallowed be thy name.
Thy kingdom come.
Thy will be done,
on earth as it is in heaven.
Give us this day our daily bread.
And forgive us our sins,
as we forgive those who sin against us.
And lead us not into temptation,
but deliver us from evil.
For thine is the kingdom,
the power, and the glory, for ever and ever.
Amen.

(Matt. 6:9–13; Luke 11:2–4)

25

Our Father, who art in heaven.

The Commandments tell us what God demands of us, and the Creed, in turn, relates what he gives to us. In the Lord's Prayer we ask that God would give us daily strength to obey his will and to believe in him.

Life's trials drive us to pray for help and strength from outside of us. A faltering prayer, even without words, is the Holy Spirit working in us and also our turning to the Creator, the giver of life.

Jesus himself taught us the Lord's Prayer. When we pray the words Jesus taught us, we ask for matters in God's will. We confess the fact that God knows what is good for us and what we really need.

Faith in the Heavenly Father gives us the courage to pray with freedom and security. We admit to our complete dependency on almighty God while approaching our beloved Father. We can be confident that he hears us and takes care of our entire lives.

■ The Lord is my shepherd, I shall not want. (Ps. 23:1)

■ For all who are led by the Spirit of God are children of God. For you did not receive a spirit of slavery to fall back into fear, but you have received a spirit of adoption. When we cry, "Abba! Father! it is that very spirit bearing witness with our spirit that we are children of God." (Rom. 8:14—16)

■ For us there is one God, the Father, from whom are all things and for whom we exist, and one Lord, Jesus Christ, through whom are all things and through whom we exist. (1 Cor. 8:6)

Our Father, who art in heaven.

WHAT DOES THIS MEAN? ANSWER:

Here God would encourage us to believe that he is truly our Father and we are truly his children in order that we may approach him boldly and confidently in prayer, even as beloved children approach their dear father.

(Martin Luther: Small Catechism)

26

THE FIRST PETITION

Hallowed be thy name.

In prayer we approach the holy God. Prayer is not a conversation between two equal partners but that of a small human being humbling herself before the great and holy God.

The name of God expresses who we believe in and who our God is. We do not believe in the unknown forces of destiny but in a personal God who makes himself manifest and who is encountered in faith.

Since God is holy, so is his name. The hallowing of God's name means that we honor God in all and gratefully accept everything that he has done for us.

The holiness of God binds us to faith and life in harmony with his word. As our baptism took place in the name of the Triune God, our entire lives are to be led honoring God. In the Lord's Prayer, we ask that God would guide all our words and deeds and that his name would be made holy among all nations.

■ You shall not make wrongful use of the name of the Lord your God, for the Lord will not acquit anyone who misuses his name. (Ex. 20:7)

■ I am the Lord, that is my name; my glory I give to no other, nor my praise to idols. (Is. 42:8)

■ The angel said to Joseph: "Mary will bear a son, and you are to name him Jesus, for he will save his people from their sins." (Matt. 1:20–21)

■ In your hearts sanctify Christ as Lord. Always be ready to make your defense to anyone who demands from you an accounting for the hope that is in you. (1 Pet. 3:15)

Hallowed be thy name.

WHAT DOES THIS MEAN? ANSWER:

To be sure, God's name is holy in itself, but we pray in this petition that it may also be holy for us.

HOW IS THIS DONE? ANSWER:

When the Word of God is taught clearly and purely and we, as children of God, lead holy lives in accordance with it. Help us to do this, dear Father in heaven! But whoever teaches and lives otherwise than the Word of God teaches, profanes the name of God among us. From this preserve us, heavenly Father!

(Martin Luther: Small Catechism)

27

THE SECOND PETITION

Thy kingdom come.

God's kingdom is God's presence and work in this world and in eternity. As Omnipotent God he rules all creation even though we cannot always see his power. God has promised to hold everything in his hands, even when we only see evil increasing.

In the Lord's Prayer we ask that the Holy Spirit would dwell in our hearts and assure us of God's love. With his word and Spirit, God desires to rule our thoughts and deeds daily, so that we might believe only in him and be Christ's faithful followers.

God's kingdom is not accomplished by human effort. God alone works out all that is good. In prayer we ask that his deeds would be strengthened in the entire Church of Christ and that we could communicate his love throughout the world even now. We pray for the strength to participate in implementing the mission commandment given by Christ. God's kingdom will, however, be carried out to perfection and in a manner apparent to all only some day in eternity.

■ Jesus proclaimed: "Repent, for the kingdom of heaven has come near." (Matt. 4:17)

■ Jesus said: "But strive first for the kingdom of God and his righteousness, and all these things will be given to you as well." (Matt. 6:33)

Thy kingdom come.

WHAT DOES THIS MEAN? ANSWER:

To be sure, the kingdom of God comes of itself, without our prayer, but we pray in this petition that it may also come to us.

HOW IS THIS DONE? ANSWER:

When the heavenly Father gives us his Holy Spirit so that by his grace we may believe his holy Word and live a godly life, both here in time and hereafter forever.

(Martin Luther: Small Catechism)

28

THE THIRD PETITION

Thy will be done, on earth as it is in heaven.

God desires good things for all people. As human beings we, however, do not always comprehend how he carries out his will in the world. God's ways are unlike ours. Therefore we find it difficult to consent to his will.

Jesus also confessed that God's will was greater than his. Even in his suffering, the Son of God left his life in the Father's hands and asked that God's will be done.

As Christians we have been invited to follow our Lord and to leave all our affairs under God's governance. He has called us to his work on earth. He himself strengthens and protects us in this task.

Contrary to our doubts, we can trust that in the end God's will is for our best. We often understand God's purpose only later; at times we are left totally without an answer. While we do not comprehend God's thoughts, we hold on to the sure promises in his word.

■ Jesus said, "Abba, Father, for you all things are possible; remove this cup from me; yet, not what I want, but what you want." (Mark 14:36)

■ Jesus said: "And this is the will of him who sent me, that I should lose nothing of all that he has given me, but raise it up on the last day." (John 6:39)

■ Do not be conformed to this world, but be transformed by the renewing of your minds, so that you may discern what is the will of God—what is good and acceptable and perfect. (Rom. 12:2)

Thy will be done, on earth as it is in heaven.

WHAT DOES THIS MEAN? ANSWER:

To be sure, the good and gracious will of God is done without prayer, but we pray in this petition that it may also be done by us.

HOW IS THIS DONE? ANSWER:

When God curbs and destroys every evil counsel and purpose of the devil, of the world, and of our flesh which would hinder us from hallowing his name and prevent the coming of his kingdom, and when he strengthens us and keeps us steadfast in his Word and in faith even to the end. This is his good and gracious will.

(Martin Luther: Small Catechism)

29

THE FOURTH PETITION

Give us this day our daily bread.

All of life's gifts come from God. He lets his sun shine equally on good and evil. The good coming about as a result of human work and activity is also based on the fact that God upholds life in the world.

It is not easy to put our trust in God's generosity. Global poverty and distress make us doubt God's goodness. Bread and the other necessities of life are out of the reach of entirely too many people.

The Lord's Prayer guides us to the consideration of other people's needs and to a moderate lifestyle. God's goodness compels us to share our own goods and to see to it that all have an adequate livelihood. Even in the midst of want, we can believe that God has promised to look continually after us and all creation.

■ Give me neither poverty nor riches; feed me with the food that I need. (Prov. 30:8)

■ Jesus said: "Look at the birds of the air; they neither sow nor reap nor gather into barns, and yet your heavenly Father feeds them. Are you not of more value than they?" (Matt. 6:26)

■ Jesus said: "For the bread of God is that which comes down from heaven and gives life to the world." (John 6:33)

Give us this day our daily bread.

WHAT DOES THIS MEAN? ANSWER:

To be sure, God provides daily bread, even to the wicked, without our prayer, but we pray in this petition that God may make us aware of his gifts and enable us to receive our daily bread with thanksgiving.

WHAT IS MEANT BY DAILY BREAD? ANSWER:

Everything required to satisfy our bodily needs, such as food and clothing, house and home, fields and flocks, money and property; a pious spouse and good children, trustworthy servants, godly and faithful rulers, good government; seasonable weather, peace and health, order and honor; true friends, faithful neighbors, and the like.

(Martin Luther: Small Catechism)

30

THE FIFTH PETITION

*And forgive us our sins,
as we forgive those
who sin against us.*

In the Lord's Prayer we confess that our selfishness drives us away from God and from our neighbors. We are totally dependent on God's mercy and forgiveness. We cannot appeal to our own excellence or to our own good deeds. Every day we are compelled to ask God to have mercy on us.

Prayer is confidence that God because of Jesus Christ forgives our entire debt of sin, without reservations or conditions. Over and over again, we can put our trust in God's word, which frees us from guilt and gives us peace and joy.

God's love moves us do to others what God did for us. We cannot be merciless even to our adversaries, because God was and continues to be merciful to us.

■ As a father has compassion for his children, so the Lord has compassion for those who fear him. (Ps. 103:13)

■ Jesus said: "For if you forgive others their trespasses, your heavenly Father will also forgive you; but if you do not forgive others, neither will your Father forgive your trespasses." (Matt. 6:14–15)

■ Then his lord summoned him and said to him, "You wicked slave! I forgave you all that debt because you pleaded with me. Should you not have had mercy on your fellow slave, as I had mercy on you?" (Matt. 18:32–33)

And forgive us our debts, as we also have forgiven our debtors.

WHAT DOES THIS MEAN? ANSWER:

We pray in this petition that our heavenly Father may not look upon our sins, and on their account deny our prayers, for we neither merit nor deserve those things for which we pray. Although we may sin daily and deserve nothing but punishment, we nevertheless pray that God may grant us all things by his grace. And assuredly we on our part will heartily forgive and cheerfully do good to those who may sin against us.

(Martin Luther: Small Catechism)

31

THE SIXTH PETITION

And lead us not into temptation,

Temptations, about which the Bible and the Lord's Prayer speak, entice us to give up faith in God's goodness. Satan and our selfish being persuade us to seek refuge elsewhere than from God.

The life of a Christian is a daily struggle. We are constantly exposed to many kinds of evil: indifference, hate, envy, selfishness, and the desire for power. On the one hand we are pulled toward sin and darkness, on the other hand toward faith and light. We do not understand why God does not let us have peace from the power of evil.

Even in the most severe tribulations, we can turn our eyes to God and the promises in his word. He will give us the strength to endure trials.

■ Remember the long way that the Lord your God has led you these forty years in the wilderness, in order to humble you, testing you to know what was in your heart, whether or not you would keep his commandments. (Deut. 8:2)

■ Then his wife said to him, "Do you still persist in your integrity? Curse God, and die." But he said to her, "You speak as any foolish woman would speak. Shall we receive the good at the hand of God, and not receive the bad?" In all this Job did not sin with his lips. (Job 2:9–10)

■ Because he himself was tested by what he suffered, he is able to help those who are being tested. (Heb. 2:18)

And lead us not into temptation.

WHAT DOES THIS MEAN? ANSWER:

God tempts no one to sin, but we pray in this petition that God may so guard and preserve us that the devil, the world, and our flesh may not deceive us or mislead us into unbelief, despair, and other great and shameful sins, but that, although we may be so tempted, we may finally prevail and gain the victory.

(Martin Luther: Small Catechism)

32

THE SEVENTH PETITION

but deliver us from evil.

Every person would like to avoid evil. When we pray in the manner taught by Christ, we put our trust in God, who alone can overcome evil and deliver us from its bondage.

We cannot explain why God has allowed evil to originate or why he tolerates its power. We Christians also feel bitterly the power of evil in our lives. Even faith does not seem to free us from its destructive forces. And yet we pray that God himself would battle on our behalf. One day he will give us the final victory and liberation from all evil. God's power is greater than that of Satan.

■ The Lord will keep you from all evil; he will keep your life. The Lord will keep your going out and your coming in from this time on and forevermore. (Ps. 121:7–8)

■ Jesus said: "I am not asking you to take them out of the world, but I ask you to protect them from the evil one." (John 17:15)

■ Since, therefore, the children share flesh and blood, he himself likewise shared the same things, so that through death he might destroy the one who has the power of death, that is, the devil, and free those who all their lives were held in slavery by the fear of death. (Heb. 2:14–15)

But deliver us from evil.

WHAT DOES THIS MEAN? ANSWER:

We pray in this petition, as in a summary, that our Father in heaven may deliver us from all manner of evil, whether it affect body or soul, property or reputation, and that at last, when the hour of death comes, he may grant us a blessed end and graciously take us from this world of sorrow to himself in heaven.

(Martin Luther: Small Catechism)

33

For thine is the kingdom,
the power, and the glory,
for ever and ever.
Amen.

God has commanded us to pray, and he has promised to hear our prayers. When we ask God for what he wishes us to ask, we can be confident that he will give it to us. When we do not know how or do not have the strength to pray, we can also put our trust in the fact that the Holy Spirit will intercede on our behalf.

In the final words of the Lord's Prayer, we praise the Father and honor the Lord Jesus Christ, who taught us this prayer and who by it gathers his disciples as one. We confess that the kingdom and the glory belong to God alone in both an individual's life and in the entire world. This is where we want to add our own amen. Our praise to God begins in this world, and it will continue in heaven eternally.

■ Yours, O Lord, are the greatness, the power, the glory, the victory, and the majesty; for all that is in the heavens and on the earth is yours; yours is the kingdom, O Lord, and you are exalted as head above all. (1 Chron. 29:11)

■ Say among the nations, "The Lord is king! The world is firmly established; it shall never be moved. He will judge the peoples with equity." (Ps. 96:10)

■ Glory to God in the highest heaven, and on earth peace among those whom he favors! (Luke 2:14)

■ The Spirit helps us in our weakness; for we do not know how to pray as we ought, but that very Spirit intercedes with sighs too deep for words. And God, who searches the heart, knows what is the mind of the Spirit, because the Spirit intercedes for the saints according to the will of God. (Rom. 8:26–27)

Amen.

WHAT DOES THIS MEAN? ANSWER:

It means that I should be assured that such petitions are acceptable to our heavenly Father and are heard by him, for he himself commanded us to pray like this and promised to hear us. "Amen, amen" means "Yes, yes it shall be so."

(Martin Luther: Small Catechism)

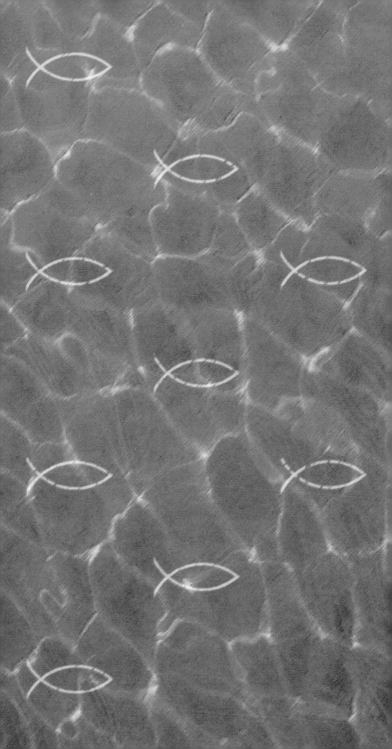

The Sacraments

BAPTISM

The Great Commission

All authority in heaven
and on earth has been given to me.
Go therefore and make disciples
of all nations,
baptizing them
in the name of the Father and
of the Son and of the Holy Spirit,
and teaching them to obey
everything that I have commanded you.
And remember, I am with you always,
to the end of the age.

(Matt. 28:18–20)

HOLY COMMUNION

The Words of Institution

Our Lord Jesus Christ,
on the night when he was betrayed,
took bread, and when he had given
thanks, he broke it,
and gave it to the disciples and said,
"Take, eat; this is my body
which is given for you.
Do this in remembrance of me."
In the same way also he took the cup,
and when he had given thanks
he gave it to them, saying,
"Drink of it, all of you.
This cup is the new covenant in my blood,
which is poured out for many
for the forgiveness of sins.
Do this, as often as you drink it,
in remembrance of me."

(Matt 26:26–29; Mark 14:22–25; Luke 22:14–20;
1 Cor. 11:23–25)

34

HOLY BAPTISM

God bestows his grace through his word and sacraments. Christ himself has instituted Baptism and the Holy Communion. They are sacraments as the word of God is joined to the elements: water, bread, and wine. The sacraments are the visible signs of grace, which we can hold on to by faith. In Baptism and Communion, Christ is present, among us, in a real and discernible manner.

Baptismal water is ordinary clean water. Joined to the word of God, it is salvatory water as it washes us clean from all sin. In his Great Commission, Christ urges us to make all nations his disciples by baptizing and teaching.

Baptism is administered in the name of the Triune God. The minister pours water on the candidate three times, saying: I baptise you in the name of the Father and of the Son and of the Holy Spirit. Appealing to God's name demonstrates that baptism is the work of God, which we do not have to earn.

■ In Christ Jesus you are all children of God through faith. As many of you as were baptized into Christ have clothed yourselves with Christ. (Gal. 3:26–27)

■ And baptism, which this prefigured, now saves you—not as a removal of dirt from the body, but as an appeal to God for a good conscience, through the resurrection of Jesus Christ. (1 Pet. 3:21)

WHAT IS BAPTISM? ANSWER:

Baptism is not merely water, but it is water used according to God's command and connected with God's Word.

WHAT IS THIS WORD OF GOD? ANSWER:

As recorded in Matthew 28:19, our Lord Christ said, "Go therefore and make disciples of all nations, baptizing them in the name of the Father and of the Son and of the Holy Spirit."

(Martin Luther: Small Catechism)

35

THE GIFT OF BAPTISM

In the sacrament of Baptism, God calls each person to be his by name. This grace is given to all, including children. Jesus ordered that children be brought to him, since the kingdom of God belongs to those who are childlike. Parents bring their children to be baptized, praying for each child with her sponsors. The value of baptism does not depend upon our attitudes, for baptism and faith are God's work in us.

Baptism makes us Christ's disciples and members of the Christian Church. Even though we are from birth under the shared guilt of humankind, in baptism we are forgiven everything, and we are then clothed in Christ's purity. The Holy Spirit regenerates us, imparting faith with which we grasp hold of the promises of baptism.

■ *Do not fear, for I have redeemed you; I have called you by name, you are mine.* (Is. 43:1)

■ *People were bringing little children to him in order that he might touch them; and the disciples spoke sternly to them. But when Jesus saw this, he was indignant and said to them, "Let the little children come to me; do not stop them; for it is to such as these that the kingdom of God belongs. Truly I tell you, whoever does not receive the kingdom of God as a little child will never enter it." And he took them up in his arms, laid his hands on them, and blessed them.* (Mark 10:13–16)

WHAT GIFTS OR BENEFITS
DOES BAPTISM BESTOW? ANSWER:

It effects forgiveness of sins, delivers from death and the devil, and grants eternal salvation to all who believe, as the Word and promise of God declare.

WHAT IS THIS WORD
AND PROMISE OF GOD? ANSWER:

As recorded in Mark 16:16, our Lord Christ said, "He who believes and is baptized will be saved; but he who does not believe will be condemned."

HOW CAN WATER PRODUCE
SUCH GREAT EFFECTS? ANSWER:

It is not the water that produces these effects, but the Word of God connected with the water, and our faith which relies on the Word of God connected with the water. For without the Word of God the water is merely water and no Baptism. But when connected with the Word of God it is a Baptism, that is, a gracious water of life and a washing of regeneration in the Holy Spirit, as St. Paul wrote to Titus (3:5–8), "He saved us by the washing of regeneration and renewal in the Holy Spirit, which he poured out upon us richly through Jesus Christ our Savior, so that we might be justified by his grace and become heirs in hope of eternal life. The saying is sure."

(Martin Luther: Small Catechism)

36

THE SIGNIFICANCE OF BAPTISM

In Baptism God joins us to Christ's death and resurrection. The Son of God died for us, and his victory over death makes us partakers of new life.

Baptism obligates us to put our trust in Christ alone and to live our lives following his example. We are, however, forced to confess every day that alongside the new creation in us lives the old selfish person who pulls us away from God.

Baptism, once received, carries us through our entire lives. The covenant of Baptism is steadfast even when our faith waivers. When we take refuge in baptismal grace, we need not do penance in our own power. The Holy Spirit weeds selfishness from us daily, awakening new faith and love in us. Baptism gives us the courage both to live and to die.

■ Do you not know that all of us who have been baptized into Christ Jesus were baptized into his death? Therefore we have been buried with him by baptism into death, so that, just as Christ was raised from the dead by the glory of the Father, so we too might walk in newness of life. (Rom. 6:3–4)

■ Let us approach with a true heart in full assurance of faith, with our hearts sprinkled clean from an evil conscience and our bodies washed with pure water. Let us hold fast to the confession of our hope without wavering, for he who has promised is faithful. (Heb. 10:22–23)

WHAT DOES SUCH BAPTIZING WITH WATER SIGNIFY? ANSWER:

It signifies that the old Adam in us, together with all sins and evil lusts, should be drowned by daily sorrow and repentance and be put to death, and that the new man should come forth daily and rise up, cleansed and righteous, to live forever in God's presence.

WHERE IS THIS WRITTEN? ANSWER:

In Romans 6:4, St. Paul wrote, "We were buried therefore with him by baptism into death, so that as Christ was raised from the dead by the glory of the Father, we too might walk in newness of life."

(Martin Luther: Small Catechism)

37

HOLY COMMUNION

The Holy Communion or the Sacrament of the Altar is the holy supper instituted by Christ. In it he gives us his body and his blood to eat and drink.

The bread and wine of the Holy Communion is Christ's real body and blood. Even though we cannot comprehend this mystery, we can be confident in the Savior's own words written in the holy Bible. The night before his death Jesus shared with his disciples the bread he had blessed and said, "This is my body." In the same way he also gave wine, which according to his own words is the blood of the covenant, his own blood. Faithful to these words of Jesus, we celebrate the Holy Communion in his memory.

The altar is the place of God's presence, around which the Christian congregation gathers to pray and give thanks to God, to hear his word and to receive the sacrament of the Holy Communion. The public and communal divine service gives us strength for our lives and activities.

■ Jesus said: "Those who eat my flesh and drink my blood abide in me, and I in them." (John 6:56)

■ They devoted themselves to the apostles' teaching and fellowship, to the breaking of bread and the prayers. (Acts 2:42)

■ The cup of blessing that we bless, is it not a sharing in the blood of Christ? The bread that we break, is it not a sharing in the body of Christ? Because there is one bread, we who are many are one body, for we all partake of the one bread. (1 Cor. 10:16–17)

WHAT IS THE SACRAMENT OF THE ALTAR? ANSWER:

Instituted by Christ himself, it is the true body and blood of our Lord Jesus Christ, under the bread and wine, given to us Christians to eat and drink.

WHERE IS IT WRITTEN? ANSWER:

The holy evangelists Matthew, Mark, and Luke, and also St. Paul, write thus: "Our Lord Jesus Christ, on the night when he was betrayed, took bread, and when he had given thanks, he broke it, and gave it to the disciples and said, 'Take, eat; this is my body which is given for you. Do this in remembrance of me.' In the same way also he took the cup, after supper, and when he had given thanks he gave it to them, saying, 'Drink of it, all of you. This cup is the new covenant in my blood, which is poured out for many for the forgiveness of sins. Do this, as often as you drink it, in remembrance of me.' "

(Martin Luther: Small Catechism)

38

THE GIFT OF THE HOLY COMMUNION

In the Holy Communion we commemorate Jesus' death on the cross. On the cross of Calvary, Jesus Christ, the only begotten Son of God, the Lamb of God, shed his blood and died on behalf of the entire world. In the sacrament of Christ's body and blood, Christ, offered as a sacrifice on the cross, gives himself to us.

The gift of the Holy Communion, that is the forgiveness of sins, is given us in the words spoken to us as we receive the elements: "given for you." When we believe these words and receive the bread and the wine, we enjoy a spiritual meal which renews our lives and adds to the love in us for our neighbors. The Holy Communion joins us to Christ and to one another. It is celebrated together with the heavenly host and all the saints.

By enjoying the Holy Communion, we remain in Christ and he remains in us. The body of Christ, the bread of life, nourishes and strengthens the spiritual life begun in Baptism. The blood of Christ, the remedy of immortality, heals us and offers us eternal life. The Holy Communion heralds the heavenly feast to which Christ will one day gather all his own.

■ But he was wounded for our transgressions, crushed for our iniquities; upon him was the punishment that made us whole, and by his bruises we are healed. (Is. 53:5)

■ When he was at the table with them, he took bread, blessed and broke it, and gave it to them. Then their eyes were opened, and they recognized him; and he vanished from their sight. (Luke 24:30–31)

■ Jesus said to them, "I am the bread of life. Whoever comes to me will never be hungry, and whoever believes in me will never be thirsty." (John 6:35)

WHAT IS THE BENEFIT OF SUCH EATING AND DRINKING? ANSWER:

We are told in the words "for you" and "for the forgiveness of sins." By these words the forgiveness of sins, life, and salvation are given to us in the sacrament, for where there is forgiveness of sins, there are also life and salvation.

HOW CAN BODILY EATING AND DRINKING PRODUCE SUCH GREAT EFFECTS? ANSWER:

The eating and drinking do not in themselves produce them, but the words "for you" and "for the forgiveness of sins." These words, when accompanied by the bodily eating and drinking, are the chief thing in the sacrament, and he who believes these words has what they say and declare: the forgiveness of sins.

(Martin Luther: Small Catechism)

39

THE SIGNIFICANCE OF
THE HOLY COMMUNION

In accordance with Christ's word, each communicant receives his body and blood. The essence of the Holy Communion is grounded in Christ's work, not the person administering Communion or its recipient. The prerequisite for proper partaking of the Holy Communion is faith, which means putting our trust in Christ's word. Even with a fragile faith, we can take solace in Christ's body and blood having been given just for us.

We can come to the communion table even if we do not fully understand its significance. Christ's body and blood must, however, be separated from other eating and drinking. The Holy Communion is to be explained to participating children in an appropriate manner. Confirmed members of the congregation can independently come to the Communion since they have been given instruction concerning the Holy Communion; further, they have confessed the common faith of the church.

The Holy Communion is meant for every Christian. When we search ourselves, we are forced to admit that we are full of unbelief and lovelessness. We need this holy supper. Christ invites to his table especially those who feel they are sinners.

■ Jesus said: "Come to me, all you that are weary and are carrying heavy burdens, and I will give you rest." (Matt. 11:28)

■ Examine yourselves, and only then eat of the bread and drink of the cup. For all who eat and drink without discerning the body, eat and drink judgment against themselves. (1 Cor. 11:28–29)

*WHO, THEN, RECEIVES
THIS SACRAMENT WORTHILY? ANSWER:*

Fasting and bodily preparation are a good external discipline, but he is truly worthy and well prepared who believes these words: "for you" and "for the forgiveness of sins." On the other hand, he who does not believe these words, or doubts them, is unworthy and unprepared, for the words "for you" require truly believing hearts.

(Martin Luther: Small Catechism)

The Bible,
Confession, Prayer,
and the Benediction

40

THE BIBLE

God speaking to us

The Bible is the Holy Book for Christians. In the Old and New Testaments we read about God's deeds and about his love toward all people. Just as in Christ, the Bible has the human and the divine intermingled. In the Bible God himself speaks to us in human language.

As God's word, the Bible examines and tries us, revealing our selfishness and unbelief. Like a mirror, it shows what we are really like. At the same time it turns our eyes to the Savior, who did for us what we ourselves are incapable of doing. Christ and his love toward us are the key to understanding the Bible.

Since we cannot build our lives on our own merits, time and time again we have to rely on the promise found in God's word. When we read or hear God's word, the Holy Spirit kindles in us a renewed trust and courage.

■ Your word is a lamp to my feet and a light to my path. (Ps. 119:105)

■ No prophecy ever came by human will, but men and women moved by the Holy Spirit spoke from God. (2 Pet. 1:21)

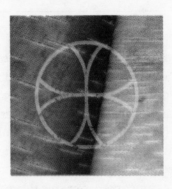

41

CONFESSION

The word of forgiveness to us

In the confession God forgives us all our sins. In the light of his Commandments and word, we are forced to admit that we have transgressed against him in thought, word, and deed. God's love gives us the courage to confess our guilt.

We can confess our sins to God in the common worship service, in private confession, or in silent prayer. We can confess our sins to a pastor or to another Christian when our conscience bothers us, giving us no peace. The one who hears our confession is bound to confidentiality as to what was said in private confession.

In the confession the words of forgiveness and consolation that we hear are ours to hold on to. The words of absolution are certain, for they are, according to God's promise, his own words. God wipes away all our sins on account of Christ. His unconditional pardon makes us free and gives us a good conscience.

■ Then I acknowledged my sin to you, and I did not hide my iniquity; I said, "I will confess my transgressions to the Lord," and you forgave the guilt of my sin. (Ps. 32:5)

■ Jesus breathed on them and said: "Receive the Holy Spirit. If you forgive the sins of any, they are forgiven them; if you retain the sins of any, they are retained." (John 20:22–23)

WHAT IS CONFESSION? ANSWER:

Confession consists of two parts. One is that we confess our sins. The other is that we receive absolution or forgiveness from the confessor as from God himself, by no means doubting but firmly believing that our sins are thereby forgiven before God in heaven.

WHAT SINS SHOULD WE CONFESS? ANSWER:

Before God we should acknowledge that we are guilty of all manner of sins, even those of which we are not aware, as we do in the Lord's Prayer. Before the confessor, however, we should confess only those sins of which we have knowledge and which trouble us.

WHAT ARE SUCH SINS? ANSWER:

Reflect on your condition in the light of the Ten Commandments: whether you are a father or mother, a son or daughter, a master or servant; whether you have been disobedient, unfaithful, lazy, ill-tempered, or quarrelsome; whether you have harmed anyone by word or deed; and whether you have stolen, neglected, or wasted anything, or done other evil.

(Martin Luther: Small Catechism)

42

PRAYER

The heart speaking with God

Prayer is a human way of being and living before the face of God. It is as natural and necessary to our spiritual lives as is breathing to our bodies. God sees us every moment. We can talk to him and he to us.

Prayer can be sighing without words, reading a familiar prayer, or free-flowing talk to God. We can pray alone, with others, or together with the whole congregation. We ask help for ourselves or others and thank God for the gifts we have received. Prayer also means honoring God, recognizing his omnipotence and pausing before his examining and loving eyes. God himself urges us to pray when we are in need, and to trust in his help.

The evening prayer we learned as children helps us to put our trust in God throughout our lives. Morning prayers and grace at table are also small worship services in our everyday lives. As the day dawns we thank God for his protection over us at night and ask for his blessings on our daily activities. At meals we thank him for his goodness. In the evening we ask him to forgive our sins, and we leave ourselves and one another in his care.

■ Do not worry about anything, but in everything by prayer and supplication with thanksgiving let your requests be made known to God. And the peace of God, which surpasses all understanding, will guard your hearts and your minds in Christ Jesus. (Phil. 4:6–7)

■ First of all, then, I urge that supplications, prayers, intercessions, and thanksgivings be made for everyone, for kings and all who are in high positions, so that we may lead a quiet and peaceable life in all godliness and dignity. This is right and is acceptable in the sight of God our Savior, who desires everyone to be saved and to come to the knowledge of the truth. (1 Tim. 2:1–4)

MORNING PRAYER

In the morning when you get up, make the sign of the holy cross and say:

In the name of the Father and of the Son and of the Holy Spirit. Amen.

Then, kneeling or standing, repeat the Creed and the Lord's Prayer. If you choose, you may also say this little prayer:

I thank you, my heavenly Father, through Jesus Christ, your dear Son, that you have kept me this night from all harm and danger; and I pray that you would keep me this day also from sin and every evil, that all my doings and life may please you. For into your hands I commend myself, my body and soul, and all things. Let your holy angel be with me, that the evil foe may have no power over me. Amen.

Then go joyfully to your work, singing a hymn, like that of the Ten Commandments, or whatever your devotion may suggest.

(Martin Luther: Small Catechism)

EVENING PRAYER

In the evening when you go to bed, make the sign of the holy cross and say:

In the name of the Father and of the Son and of the Holy Spirit. Amen.

Then kneeling or standing, repeat the Creed and the Lord's Prayer. If you choose, you may also say this little prayer:

I thank you, my heavenly Father, through Jesus Christ, your dear Son, that you have graciously kept me this day; and I pray that you would forgive me all my sins where I have done wrong, and graciously keep me this night. For into your hands, I commend myself, my body and soul, and all things. Let your holy angel be with me, that the evil foe may have no power over me. Amen.

Then go to sleep at once and in good cheer.

(Martin Luther: Small Catechism)

ASKING A BLESSING

The eyes of all look to you, O Lord, and you give them their food at the proper time. You open your hand and satisfy the desires of every living thing.

It is to be observed that "satisfying the desires of every living thing" means that all creatures receive enough to eat to make them joyful and of good cheer. Greed and anxiety about food prevent such satisfaction.

Then shall be said the Lord's Prayer and the following:

Lord God, heavenly Father, bless us and these your gifts which we receive from your bountiful goodness, through Jesus Christ, our Lord. Amen.

RETURNING THANKS

Give thanks to the Lord, for he is good, his love endures forever. He gives food to every creature. He provides food for the cattle and for the young ravens when they call. His pleasure is not in the strength of the horse, nor his delight in the legs of a man; the Lord delights in those who fear him, who put their hope in his unfailing love.

Then shall be said the Lord's Prayer and the following:

We thank you, Lord God, heavenly Father, for all your benefits, through Jesus Christ, our Lord, who lives and reigns with you and the Holy Spirit forever and ever. Amen.

(Martin Luther: *Small Catechism*)

43

THE BENEDICTION

The Lord bless you and keep you;
the Lord make his face to shine
upon you, and be gracious to you:
The Lord lift up his countenance
upon you, and give you peace.
In the name of the Father, Son,
and Holy Spirit.
Amen.

(Num. 6:24–26)

We live leaning on God's blessings every day. His goodness and grace surround us. God protects our lives even though we do not always know the paths of his love. He gives us inner peace, which supports us even amidst all the brokenness in life. Trusting in God's blessing, some day we can die.

When we bless one another or ask blessings for ourselves, we can be confident that the Triune God turns to us and is with us.

■ *The grace of the Lord Jesus Christ, the love of God, and the communion of the Holy Spirit be with all of you.* (2 Cor. 13:13)

GENERAL INDEX

The references are to sections.